ANTS

INSECTS

James P. Rowan

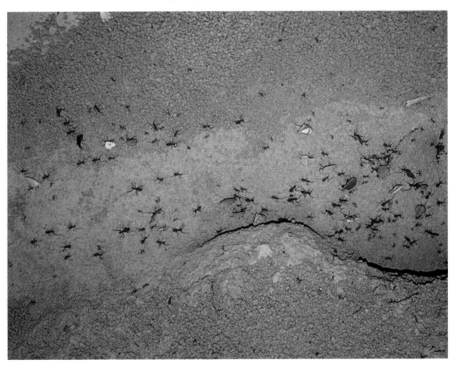

The Rourke Corporation, Inc.
Vero Beach, Florida 32964

Edited by Sandra A. Robinson

PHOTO CREDITS
© James P. Rowan: cover, pages 4, 7, 10, 15, 17, 18, 21; © Frank
Balthis: title page; © Jerry Hennen: page 8; © Lynn M. Stone:
pages 12, 13

Library of Congress Cataloging-in-Publication Data

Rowan, James P.
   Ants / by James P. Rowan.
      p.   cm. — (The Insect discovery library)
   Includes index.
   Summary: An introduction to the physical characteristics, habits,
and behavior of ants.
   ISBN 0-86593-289-1
   1. Ants—Juvenile literature. [1. Ants.] I. Title. II. Series.
QL568.F7R85   1993
595.79'6—dc20   89-32924
                                                          CIP
                                                          AC

TABLE OF CONTENTS

ANTS

Ants are one of nearly a million kinds, or **species,** of **insects.** Scientists have divided insects into groups. Each group is made up of insects that are alike in certain ways. Ants are grouped together with bees and wasps.

Like their relatives, ants have mouthparts that chew. Some ants can also sting.

Though most ants do not have wings, young queen and male ants have wings for a short time.

This carpenter ant and its cousins are chewing insects related to bees

ANT COLONIES

Many ants live together in a large group called a **colony.** Some colonies have thousands of ants.

Most of the ants in a colony are workers. Workers collect food for the colony and care for the young ants.

Each colony has a queen. She is larger than the workers and can live 10 years or more. The queen is the mother of all of the other ants in the colony.

A few species have ant soldiers to protect the colony from enemies.

Inside an Illinois ant colony, adults care for the egg, larva and pupa stages of their offspring

WHERE ANTS LIVE

Most ants, such as little black ants, live below the ground in tunnels, or **galleries.** They sometimes build mounds around the opening to the nest. The mounds help keep rainwater from flooding the galleries.

Some ants live in wood. Large, black carpenter ants live in dead trees and wooden buildings. They do not eat wood as termites do. They chew through it to make their galleries.

Ants swarm atop their colony's
entrance mound in South Dakota

KINDS OF ANTS

More than 2,500 species of ants live throughout the world. The leaf-cutting ant of Central America is one of the most unusual. Some of the workers go into the forest and chew pieces of leaves from plants and trees. As the pieces fall to the ground, other workers carry them back to the nest.

Termites are sometimes called white ants. Termites are not really ants, although they have workers, soldiers and a queen.

A leaf-cutting ant in Mexico hauls its prize — a piece of leaf

A tiny, armored knight, the horned lizard lives only on a diet of ants

*The armadillo, another predator of ants, has a long, narrow snout
that is perfect for ant-eating*

WHAT ANTS EAT

Ants eat many different foods. Harvester ants like to eat the seeds of different kinds of grasses. Some ants eat other kinds of insects.

Most ants like to eat sweets. You may have shared a picnic with ants!

Some ants even grow their own food! Leaf-cutting ants chew up leaf pieces and make them into fertilizer. A special kind of **fungus** that the ants like to eat grows from the fertilizer.

A pair of ants drag their insect prey to the colony

EGG TO ADULT

An ant begins life as a tiny egg laid by the queen. The egg hatches into a wormlike **larva.** The larva is cared for by worker ants.

When the larva is fully grown, it forms the third stage, or **pupa.** In this stage the ant does not eat or move. It is slowly changing into the fourth stage, the adult.

An adult ant moves an ant larva inside the colony

ANT ENEMIES

Many kinds of animals like to eat ants. One is the anteater of South America. It has a long, sticky tongue to catch the ants in their tunnels, and large claws to tear open ant nests. Armadillos and bears also like ants. The horned lizard of the southwestern United States eats only ants!

The antlion is an insect that eats ants.

Tough little crab spiders are among the ant eaters of backyards and gardens

ANT HABITS

Ants sometimes walk single file. Each ant follows a trail of scent made by the one ahead. They smell the scent with their **antennas.**

Another curious habit of ants is guarding aphids. Aphids are small insects that make a sweet liquid called honeydew. Ants love honeydew. Some ants protect aphids from their enemies. Ants may even take aphids into the ant nest on cold days.

Ants are caretakers of aphids

ANTS AND PEOPLE

A few kinds of ants go where they are not wanted. Then they become **pests.**

Sometimes ants crawl or chew into people's homes. They come looking for food. People don't enjoy having ants in their kitchens.

Fire ants are another ant pest. They live in large underground colonies in the southern United States. When someone disturbs their colony, fire ants stream out. Their bites burn like fire.

Glossary

antennas (an TEN uhz) — whiplike structures on the heads of insects and several other boneless animals

colony (KAHL uh nee) — a group of nesting animals of the same kind

fungus (FUN gus) — a kingdom of plantlike organisms that includes mushrooms

galleries (GAL er eez) — long tunnels made by ants for living and food storage

insect (IN sekt) — a large group of little animals without backbones (invertebrates) that have three pairs of legs and three basic body parts: head, thorax and abdomen

larva (LAR vuh) — the stage of insect development between egg and pupa

pest (PEST) — something that goes or grows where it is not wanted

pupa (PYU puh) — the stage of development between larva and adult when the insect is inactive

species (SPEE sheez) — within a group of closely-related animals, such as ants, one certain kind or type (*leaf-eating* ant)

INDEX